HELLENISM AND
THE MODERN WORLD

HELLENISM
AND THE
MODERN WORLD

*Six Talks on the
Radio-diffusion Française
and the BBC*

BY

GILBERT MURRAY, O.M.

LONDON
GEORGE ALLEN & UNWIN LTD
RUSKIN HOUSE MUSEUM STREET

*Printed in Great Britain
in* 11 *on* 13*-point Baskerville type
by Unwin Brothers Limited
Woking and London*

PREFACE

THESE TALKS were given first on the Radio-diffusion Française in 1952 and repeated, with some revision, on the BBC Home Service in April–May 1953. In the meantime, however, I had listened to those fascinating Reith Lectures on "The World and the West" with which Arnold Toynbee shook us all from our dogmatic slumbers. I thought at first that I should have to make some changes, or at least some withdrawals of rash statements, in my script. But it was not necessary. Even in that small part of his vast canvas where we were dealing with the same subject our focus of interest was different. I was trying to trace the special development of that 'Christian' or 'Hellenic' civilization to which we peoples of Europe and the English-speaking world historically belong, and to consider how, amid multifarious 'barbarian' influences it may still preserve or even raise its traditional standards, and continue to set to the whole world an example of what is meant by civilization. Mr. Toynbee carefully abstained from any such self-admiring prejudice, observing that naturally every nation thought its own ways the best, and merely noting objectively the 'aggressions' and 're-actions' between them. One lesson at least which we of the West may learn from Mr. Toynbee's book will be to take great care, when we are bringing help to some 'barbarian' or 'less advanced' nation in need, that what we think of as generous help may not seem to the recipient more like contemptuous almsgiving or even arrogant interference.

I hope I am not blind to the defects of our western civilization or oblivious of the terrible wrongs done throughout history by the dominant races of mankind to those who stood in their way. Yet I feel strongly that the Western Community, with all its faults and vulgarities, and with all that it still has to learn from certain Eastern nations, is nevertheless, in virtue of its Hellenic and Christian heritage, called upon to lead the world. "The present is hard and the future veiled"; and we have a very great civilization to lose or save. It is not an effete or corrupt generation that responded with such instant enthusiasm to the vow of dedication and service undertaken by our young queen; not a cynical world which, after the disastrous failure of its hopes in the League of Nations, has so almost unanimously pledged itself again to follow the same practical ideal; not a hardened or unrepentant community which is pouring out such a vast flood of charity and remedial measures from every possible source, personal, social, religious and governmental, in its longing to redeem the wrongs

of the Second World War. The silent under-
currents of human feeling are, I believe, far nobler
and in the long run more important than the
much publicized conflicts of national or sectional
ambition. Of course all is in danger. But I see
no reason to doubt that our Christian or Hellenic
civilization is on the right road; certainly no
reason to lower our traditional standards or
abate our old courage.

G. M.

CONTENTS

I

THE CHRISTIAN TRADITION: ROME, JERUSALEM, ATHENS

EVERY CIVILIZATION has its roots in the past, and Europe has a great civilization of which we Europeans are all extremely conscious, though we hardly know what name to give it. We sometimes say 'Christian', sometimes 'Hellenic'. Of course, historically, we all have millions of ancestors: Europe is the product of multitudes of different nations and histories; yet it is surprising how little permanent effect most of them have had. Allowing for a vigorous influence from the North and a little, mostly unconscious, from the East, our vital inheritance seems really to come from three particular cities: Athens, Jerusalem and Rome.

The Roman influence is everywhere. It is by far the most visible and striking; but in almost every case, when we look beneath the surface, the real moving power is Greek. Our Latin alphabet is really Greek, our Roman Law Greek in origin, our political ideas almost entirely Greek. We even describe the tradition as 'Hellenic' because, as the Roman poet says, *"Graecia capta ferum victorem cepit"*: "captured Greece made her rude conqueror captive". Greek culture was moving on much the same lines as Rome, but happened to be more advanced; also, Greece had from the most primitive times an extraordinary command of language: at a stage when other peoples could scarcely mumble, the Greeks were clearly articulate. They could think clearly; they could explain and teach.

In the ordinary regions of scientific knowledge Rome had simply to follow the lead of Greece. She had to learn from Greece her architecture, her field measurements, her seamanship and navigation, her medicine, her geography, geometry, astronomy and mathematics in general. We do not notice our dependence on Greece and Rome in such things, because discoveries in science, however glorious to the discoverer and important to society, are quickly surpassed by further discoveries and made obsolete. But in the region of things that are not ever surpassed, the regions of imagination and aspiration, Greece had the same unquestioned lead. A Roman with a love of poetry in the first or second century B.C. found abundance of magnificent Greek poetry to read, and very little in his own language or elsewhere. When Virgil's genius sought expression, it found it in the sort of pastorals that Theocritus wrote, in the poems about fields and crops and bees that Hesiod and Arâtus wrote, or in some part of the great heroic or romantic tradition expressed by so many Greek poets from Homer to Apollonius. Horace, a great original poet himself, can give no more emphatic advice to a young poet than to turn over his Greek models night and day. When Lucretius wanted to find the true secret of the universe, he could only go to a Greek philosopher for it; when he wanted the proper technique for expressing it in such a way as to move mankind, he went to Greek poets. The philosophy which moved the Romans most was, characteristically, that which was concerned with practice and told men and statesmen what to do. It was ethics, politics and, to some extent, religion. That sort of thing was only to be found in Greek writers. The Latin language had not even the necessary vocabulary, until great masters of language like Cicero invented the suitable words and could proceed to translate and explain. It is interesting to notice that Cicero, the first Roman philosopher, translates from the Greek, but in less than two centuries later the chief Roman philosopher of that time, Marcus Aurelius, actually writes in Greek. Roman civilization, as it became more perfect, became more Hellenic, and as it decayed tried to grasp tightly the bits of Hellenism that it could still hold.

The Romans were wonderful governors, probably the best there had ever been. They had courage, conscience and a sense of justice; but otherwise they were rough, practical men. If we look for the specific heritage which the Roman example has left for modern civilization to maintain or to recover, we shall find, I think, two great institutions: a united religion and a united civilization. In saying united, I mean world-wide or 'œcumenical' in the limited, ancient sense—that is, covering what they called the *oecúmené*, the 'inhabited' or civilized world as known to the Romans. The united civilization was attained by deliberate effort, by military conquest and effective government. It lasted with varying degrees of success for some centuries. It is above all things what we are now striving to recover. The united religion came about almost unconsciously, and indeed reluctantly, in response to the primordial cravings of human society, and has lasted on in great strength to the present day.

To discuss the effort for political unity would take us too far afield; but the movement towards unity in religion is instructive to trace, and perhaps suggests to us a great problem for our own future.

Ancient religions were never intolerant, but were always extremely local. You had your own gods and could fairly neglect other people's gods—unless indeed you happened to be in their territory, when of course you must show them proper respect. Man's whole life in an agricultural age depended on the annual food-supply; so the local gods were mostly agricultural. Each little settlement had its divine protectors; almost always a local Earth-Mother and a divine Son or Young King, who brought the new vegetation and went through the whole annual process of birth, death and resurrection. There was of course also a great Father, to rule and protect and do justice, but he was farther off in the sky. The Son was nearer; he came from the union of Sky and Earth, the son of a god and a mortal woman.

As the rule of Rome spread and became a unity, her old local cults could not be expected to serve the needs of nations far off who had never seen Rome. A religion was needed for the whole Roman Empire; and Roman statesmen, though not as a rule much interested in religious speculations, had to attend to it. The subject peoples might of course go on worshipping their own gods as much as they liked, but they must somehow give honour and worship to the gods of Rome. Experiments

were tried with *Dea Roma*, the Goddess Rome;
but it did not act very well. It was somehow
too artificial for a real religion. Then, on the
analogy of oriental kings, the Emperor himself
was deified. He did not insist on being actually
worshipped, and some Emperors ventured to
make jokes about their supposed deification.
It was enough if his special authority was
recognized; enough if people would, as a sign
of loyalty, burn a little incense to him. If any
nation refused that, it was suspicious; it must
mean that they had some sinister religion of
their own, with gods who hated Rome, or
perhaps hated all mankind except their chosen
people. All normal Roman citizens wanted
some common worship. Historians have noticed
as one of the weaknesses of the Graeco-Roman
world that the only sphere in which they showed
much original thought was that where philosophy
merges into religion. Could not the philosophers
devise a suitable world religion? They tried
and tried, but their systems were too highly
intellectual, too much based on reason. How
could the mass of men understand them? And
a world religion must be based on man's
instinctive wants and fears, not on his arguments.
The old City-state had by now become obsolete
as an independent unit of government, so the
old City-state cults had become obsolete also.

The way was open for some common religion which would unite all the *oecûmené*, all the inhabited world. It could not of course be something entirely new. It must be based on something already existing in the Mediterranean peoples. It must somehow satisfy the old primordial desire of the human heart for something human or friendly behind the mass of dead phenomena—for a Father to protect and to do justice, for a Mother who could love and pity her children; and in all agricultural peoples for a spring vegetation god, a saviour born of Sky and Earth. At one time it looked as if the Persian–Babylonian cult of Mithras, the faithful Saviour who gave his life in sacrifice for his people, might become the religion of the Empire. It was strong in the imperial armies and was ready to make a mystical identification of the reigning Emperor with the *Sol Invictus Mithras*. But something shook its prestige: perhaps its failure to resist the attacks of the northern barbarians; perhaps its lack of emotional appeal compared with the Isis–Osiris cult of Egypt, or the cults of those Anatolian communities which put first a Divine Mother, with her son and her consort less emphasized. But the ultimate success, permanent and undoubted, fell to the combination of Jewish and Greek worship called Christianity.

B

The two had influenced one another for a long time. The Old Testament was Hebrew, but parts of it showed Greek influence; the Apocrypha was mostly Greek or mostly extant in Greek; the New Testament was all in Greek, with such Aramaic sources as there may have been soon forgotten or obliterated. Coming from the Jews and the subject peoples of the eastern provinces, it became in part a cry of human suffering, a religion of the poor and oppressed. A wonderful blend it was; and we have, of course, a wonderful account of its making. Paul, the Hellenistic Jew, who must have been quite familiar with the idea of a World-Saviour, rather than a Jewish Messiah, seemed suddenly, after long meditation in the wilderness, to see that the World-Saviour had actually been born of woman and lived and known sacrifice and resurrection, in the person of Jesus of Nazareth. St. Paul was a Jew as well as a Greek-speaking Roman citizen. One can see how his old Hebrew wine-flasks are almost bursting with the new wine of his Greek mysticism. But the religious cravings of the world to which he preached not only accepted him, but soon went far beyond him. They craved for a divine Mother as well as a Father; they had always had her and could not give her up: indeed, without her, how could they have their divine Saviour Son? The Jews in Jerusalem, so proud of their pure monotheism, might violently reject the transformation; but the Hellenistic world was crying out for it, or something like it.

The quest for this universal religion produced a phenomenon previously unknown, or almost unknown, in antiquity: religious strife and persecution. As long as every locality or sect was free to have its own religion there was no particular reason to fight; but as soon as a universal claim was made there was a clash between the claimants. Chapels of Mithras have been unearthed full of corpses apparently burned to death by a rival sect. Besides, the universal claim naturally provoked resistance; and resistance gave rise to suspicion. Why was it that Jews or Christians refused to worship the gods? Because they were atheists? or because the Jews, as their Bible confessed, 'abhorred' all gentile gods and all gentiles? Only after long and fierce conflicts did the Graeco-Roman world at last find what it sought in an œcumenical Church, which survived the wrecks of empires and combined the aspirations of Hebrew and Hellene. Thus Rome gave us the framework, as Athens and Jerusalem on the whole gave the inner content of our living Christian civilization.

II

HISTORICAL HELLENISM
THE REAL GREECE

WHAT WAS IT really like, this Hellenic civilization that had such a penetrating effect, that made Rome turn Hellenic, made Hebrew religion turn Hellenic, and has left the word 'Hellenism' as a sort of ideal heritage to many nations? Like all ideals, that ideal 'Hellenism' is of course a good deal different from the reality on which it is based. Our own modern civilization, a true child of Hellenism, at first sight seems extremely unlike that of ancient Greece. Any ancient Greek would feel far more at home in an untouched Polynesian island than in London or New York. Ours is an age of highly organized material civilization, accustomed to complete security in daily life, an age of complex machinery and mass production and of enormous governmental strength. The civilization of Greece, even of the Athenians at their most prosperous period, was startlingly unlike this. The arm of their government was neither long nor strong; within a day's walk from the Athens of Pericles

and Socrates you would find ignorant and
primitive peasants, sometimes practising barbarous rites. Only recently, says Thucydides,
had ordinary citizens felt secure enough to
go about unarmed. Greek clothes, however
gracefully worn, were little more than a sleeve-
less shirt and a blanket. They mostly went
barefoot—at any rate they called the Lydians
'soft-footed' because they habitually wore shoes.
They had no great roads, such as the Persians
had; no drainage system like that of the Romans;
no palaces to compare with the oriental palaces.
No Greek community was ever comparable
in size, wealth, population and the like to
the great river civilizations of Egypt and Meso-
potamia. The greatness of Greece depended
on quite other qualities.

Compared with those oriental empires, a
central fact which strikes us is that in Greece
there was no divine or semi-divine Great King
in the Babylonian or Egyptian sense. For one
thing, Greek states were all on a small scale
and all more or less equal. They could, and
did, fight each other freely, but none had any
thought of establishing a vast empire over
all the rest. For another thing, Greek potentates
are always sharply warned that, however successful they may be, they are only erring mortals
and must not think they are gods. They must

not put up megalomaniac records of their
own glory; not expect people to kiss the earth
on entering their presence or to walk backwards
on leaving it; not expect to have concubines
and attendants sacrificed on their tombs; not
put people to death without trial; not kill
them by torture; not seize other men's wives
and daughters. That sort of thing is all 'barbaric',
not Hellenic. The treatment of war memorials
is particularly interesting. The Egyptians and
Assyrians put up gigantic limestone reliefs,
showing the king in superhuman size receiving
tribute from his enemies. The Assyrians showed
him making pyramids of their skulls, or leading
their kings into captivity by fish-hooks stuck
through their noses. That was the proper
barbarian way for a Great King to show his
greatness. Even the Romans long afterwards
had their rather revolting triumphs: the conqueror driving in his chariot with the spoils,
with chained prisoners dragged behind him,
their leaders to be executed after the show.
The Greek rule was utterly different. There
must be no *Hubris:* no triumph, no boasting,
no maltreatment of the enemy dead, no killing
of the prisoners of war. Furthermore, the
Greek conqueror must put up no permanent
war memorial; only what they called a 'trophy',
that is, a wooden pole and crossbar with armour

upon it, to mark the site of the victory; a monument which by a rule of honour the conqueror must never repair and the conquered never pull down. Both must allow it gradually to break up and sink into the earth as the memory of the old evils faded. Man must remember his insecurity and beware of the fatal delusions of *Hubris*.

On the whole, in most ancient communities, the duty of man was pretty clearly prescribed by long-established tradition. It consisted of obedience to a great king, or to a god in the image of a great king, and the observance of a great number of traditional *taboos.* Think of the Book of Leviticus, with its elaborate list of *taboos* and rules of behaviour, the insistence on circumcision and the 'abhorring' of those tribes which did not practise it; think, even, of the detailed rules in Hammurabi's great code. In Greece we meet here and there fragmentary relics of such *taboos:* sects which abstain from beans or from animal flesh, or families which practise some special form of worship. But they seem to be merely relics of systems that have long passed away, of tribes and ancestral communities that have been broken up. In private life, indeed, a man's duty might be summed up in three commands: to obey the gods, to honour his parents, and to do no injustice to strangers. But in public political life there was no traditional head of the family, or tribal chief taking his place; a man's duty was not to his ancestral or tribal chief, but to the *Polis* and its Laws; and even those Laws were recognized as man-made, to be criticized if they were not Just.

Early Greek origins are obscure; but the evidence seems to point to a period of great invasions, involving a break-up of settled society, in which populations fled here and there for refuge, tribes were scattered, the sacred graves of ancestors left behind, and old customs and conventions lost. There was danger all round; the only safety was within some *Polis*, some City or circuit Wall. Each group of refugees built its own *Polis* and became an organized body behind it—not of kinsmen, but of *Politai*— 'citizens'. There remained of their old life almost nothing, except what each man could carry with him, such things as he knew or remembered—what was called his *Sophia*, his Wisdom; and such personal qualities or abilities as made him definitely good for something— his virtue or *Aretê*. The people who had taken refuge inside the *Polis* were mostly, as Strabo says, "a mixed multitude", not uniform in their traditions or customs. So they had to form new laws by agreement, often, no doubt, with a certain amount of compromise. That laid a heavy responsibility on the men themselves, the responsibility of Freedom. They had no longer an unquestioned tradition to control or guide them: they must fall back on what stores they had of active *Sophia* and *Aretê;* they must control themselves, think for themselves. They must remember not merely to be obedient to custom, which is easy, but to be really Just, which needs thought; to observe *Metron*, or Measure; to remember the rule of *Mêden Agan:* Nothing Too Much; and to avoid above all things *Hubris*, Insolence or Excess, the deadly error to which all life is subject and which leads always to a fall.

The *Polis*, or small independent City-state, seems thus to have been responsible for some of the main characteristic aims of Greek civilization: the maintenance of Freedom, and the eager pursuit of *Aretê* and *Sophia*—words which we conventionally translate by Goodness and Wisdom. But it is a Goodness which covers the qualities of a good man, a good bootmaker, a good horse or a good chisel. It is a Wisdom which ranges from craftsmanship and knowledge of mathematics to enlightened ideas and inspiration in poetry. Their craftsmanship was indeed wonderful; few ages could at all equal the actual mechanical stone-craft of the Parthenon;

but of course in science and technology their work, good as it was, has been utterly outstripped and reduced to nothing by modern discoveries. Only in philosophy, that is, the search for Truth in the great problems that still haunt mankind, and in art and poetry, that is, the impassioned vision and creation of what we vaguely call Beauty, we still, after two thousand years, are learning from them. Hellenism, more than any other civilization that we know, concentrated upon these things.

III

THE LOGOS

THE GREEKS were mocked at in antiquity for being so fond of talking. It was really their great glory. They believed in the power of the *Logos*. It was their way to settle disputes, their instrument for finding out what was true or what was fair. No other people at such an early stage of development had such a power of expressing itself. Those that had uniform tribal rules and customs did not often need to have disputes at all; if they had, the dispute became a fight. But when a 'mixed multitude' was settled as citizens in a new-built City Wall they had to come to agreement about their needs and laws and practices. They had to persuade each other; and the great instrument of persuasion, the great substitute for violence, is the *Logos*. Traditionally it is translated 'word'; but it is 'talk' or 'speech': *sermo* rather than *verbum*. It is the most characteristic word in the Greek language. I see that the New Greek Dictionary, severely compressed as it is, takes 5,500 words to explain the meaning of *Logos*. It lies at the root of philosophy, science, religion. Everything in the world has a *Logos*, it says something, means something; God himself is saying something. If we listen carefully we can understand. Also, we must preserve what wise people in the past have said, their *Logoi*. But let us consider what kind of *Logoi* the Greeks preserved, as compared with other ancient nations. The Hebrews, for instance, have left a splendid literature, but rather narrow in range. There is an account of the beginning of the world, as in Babylonian and Egyptian; there are collections of laws and taboos; there are valuable books of history, the text carefully edited again and again by the orthodox priests of Yahweh; there is a collection of songs or psalms, all religious and all in much the same style. There is also a body of literature not extant anywhere else: a collection of the oracles of the prophets—that is, of course, the prophets of Yahweh. For some reason prophecy reached a higher level of thought and expression among the Hebrews than in any other society known to us.

What of Babylon and Egypt? Babylonian literature differs from Hebrew, of course, in having the characteristics of a great imperial state. It is polytheistic. We happen to possess the remains of the library of Assurbanipal,

the last great king of Assyria; a far greater
library than anything classical Greece could
pretend to. But what are its contents? There
is Hammurabi's great code of law; there is
the cosmological epic and the epic of Gilgamesh
and a few similar poems; but in the main, a
quantity of prescribed rituals, different for
different gods and for different priests, and
adding up to a vast mass; a record of the great
deeds of the king; and then a collection of
thousands of signs and omens. It is all dominated
by religion, law, magic and astrology. Egyptian
literature, though it has some good stories and
hymns, is equally dominated by magico-religious
texts. The Book of the Dead, for instance, has
been found in more than a thousand tombs.

When we turn to Greek Literature we are
in a totally different atmosphere. The first
thing is the extraordinary variety and ease of
expression. Where Hebrew presented us with
one form of poetry—or at most two, the psalms
and the prophecies—Greek gives us the epic
and the mock epic, the philosophical poem,
the choral lyric and the personal lyric, each
class with many subdivisions; quantities of
political poems, from the reforming Solon to
the disgruntled Theognis and the revolutionary
Alcaeus; wonderful drama, both tragic and
comic; love-song, elegy and narrative. Both

Hebrew and Greek maintain a firm distinction between the half-magical language of poetry and the prose of ordinary life, but where in Hebrew there is only one fixed form of poetic language, in Greek every kind of poetry is apt to have its appropriate metre and dialect.

In prose, of course, the variety is even greater, though, curiously enough, the kind of prose that is commonest in Babylon and Egypt is absent. There are in classical times no magic texts, no books of oracles, no records of royal megalomania. Oracles are sometimes quoted, and of course magic charms must have existed, but they were not apparently considered worth preserving. There is no one impressive code of law like that of Hammurabi; but a great number of local codes, mostly the work of individual law-givers, or the result of active thought and discussion. There is history of many types, from the mere chronicle to the all-embracing *Historiē*, or 'Enquiry', of Herodotus and the masterly political history of Thucydides. Then come two forms of literature almost unknown elsewhere: philosophy and oratory. Philosophy in the most various forms, as it is based on physical science, or the needs of society, or the aspirations of ethical thought. Oratory— that is, businesslike argumentative discussion— was a natural growth from free political institu-

tions. There was no place for it in the oriental
monarchies; one can hardly imagine a discussion on foreign policy between the adherents of
Jehu and those of Jezebel, or between Nehemiah
and Sanballat the Horonite on the wisdom
of rebuilding Jerusalem; but Thucydides is
full of such debates, and, what is unparalleled
in ancient, and rare in modern, literature, both
sides seem to be understood and fairly stated.
Then there is the mass of occasional writings,
like the Old Oligarch's criticism of the Athenian
democracy, Xenophon's reminiscences, Sophron's
mimes or imaginary conversations, and the
mime's marvellous progeny, the Platonic dialogue. The variety is much greater than in any
literature before or since, until we come to
quite modern times. Neither Rome nor the
Middle Ages come near to it.

It is modern in another sense too, in the very
small part played by magic or superstition. There
must have been plenty of superstition among
the masses in Greece, and even in Athens:
that can be proved from history and is illus-
trated by Theophrastus' amusing study of The
Superstitious Man. But it was evidently looked
down upon: it was not allowed to dominate
serious literature. There is only one firmly
rooted belief of a supernatural kind, and that
one which it would be harsh to call superstition.

In poetry, history and philosophy alike, there is
an undercurrent of conviction that the whole
order of nature is somehow a moral order. The
moral law is a real fact and transgression is, by
a Law of Nature, followed by punishment. No
one can be unjust with impunity: as the proverb
says, "there are avengers for an injured dog".
Apart from this unproven faith, philosophy
in general emancipates itself from traditional
bonds with a completeness which has no parallel
before, say, the seventeenth century in France
or the eighteenth in England. As for science,
the so-called Oath of Hippocrates, the Father
of Medicine, shows an attitude which would put
to shame many practitioners for some thousand
years after. The doctor must swear "to make
no pretence of magic, never to take advantage
of a patient's sufferings or fears, but to remember
always that he enters a sick man's house as a
friend to all who dwell there".

I will not discuss the degree to which educated
Athenians in the fifth century believed in their
gods. It would be a foolish question, because
Greek religion did not operate with creeds, only
with practices. But one might say they believed
very little in the Homeric literary gods, but a
great deal in the strictly local deities who make
little show in literature but have their roots
firmly in the earth. But it seems certain that one

of the first characteristics of Greek civilization
was scepticism. There were too many *Logoi:* too
many local legends and traditions preserved;
they contradicted each other, so one could not
believe them all. There was no authoritative
orthodoxy, and seldom any censorship of a
religious kind. We find from the very outset
divergent historical traditions. Remains of local
heroic legend are often contrary to the Iliad
and Odyssey; Herodotus makes a point of
collecting and criticizing divergent versions of
the stories that he records. The first of historians,
Hecataeus, starts his book with the remarkable
outburst: "I write as seems to me true, for
the traditions (*Logoi*) of the Greeks are divergent
and absurd". In philosophy, Protagoras says
boldly: "About the gods I cannot say either
that they are or that they are not, or what
like they are". As for Heraclitus of Ephesus,
there is nothing to prevent him from saying
roundly that "much learning does not teach
sense, else it would have taught Hesiod and
Pythagoras", and adding that Homer and Archi-
lochus ought to be "whipped off the course"
for their misconduct. Imagine Jeremiah, or
even Habakkuk, who is *capable de tout*, saying
such things about Moses! More remarkable
still, perhaps, is Xenophanes, a professional
rhapsode who lived by reciting Homer: he

condemns Homer and Hesiod not only for
"attributing to the gods actions which are
disgraceful to men", but because their anthro-
pomorphic gods are ridiculous—"If cows or
lions had gods, no doubt their gods would have
the form of cows and lions. In truth god is a
spirit with no shape of that sort".

The word 'modern' is not always a term
of praise; but, in perhaps the best sense of the
word, how extraordinarily modern this is! Especially remarkable is the freedom with which the
language itself moves. Most ancient languages
are stiff; they express themselves in fixed formu-
lae; there are things they can express and things
which they cannot express. It would be almost
impossible to discuss a modern political or
philosophical problem in classical Hebrew, difficult even in Latin. But in Greek it can always
be done, unless indeed you want to talk of
things which had not been invented in Greek
times, and for which, as it happens, we generally
have to invent a Greek name—like 'telephone'
or 'cinema'. A recent Professor of Logic and
Metaphysics in Oxford, when wishing to get
some thought exactly expressed, used sometimes
to write it in Greek as being clearer than either
German or English.

Equally remarkable and almost equally modern
was the actual freedom of speech, both political

and religious. The three or four condemnations for 'impiety' like that of Socrates, which occurred in the course of a terrible and prolonged war, became famous scandals. Considering how democratic Athenian courts were, and how superstitious any Demos is when really frightened, it is a surprisingly small list. The writers quoted above do not seem to have suffered for their philosophical scepticism; Aristophanes does not seem to have lost popularity for his attacks on the war party in the midst of the war.

It does seem to have been widely recognized that, in order to reach truth or to reach justice, every thinker had to "listen to the other side". It is characteristic that Plato never dogmatizes but always approaches truth by a dialogue, an argument between different points of view, and almost always leaves at the end some doubt, some feeling that though we have got deeper we have not quite reached the complete truth. Here, too, we find the influence of the *Polis*. It was built, Aristotle says, that men might live, that they might escape from enemies and pursuers; but it goes on in order that men may "live well" and find what is really the good life. And the way to that is by the *Logos*, by thinking and discussing.

IV

A 'LIBERAL' CIVILIZATION
WRECKED BY WAR

I SAW some time ago a letter from a woman,
a cultivated and liberal-minded woman, who
had been some years in prison, first Nazi
and then Communist, where she was kept without books, till at last by some special grace
a friend was allowed to send her some. Among
the books was a Thucydides. She read the
Funeral Speech of Pericles about Athens and
almost wept: that was the sort of city which
recalled the ideals of her youth, not like any
city remaining in Europe as it now is. Of course,
the Funeral Speech is not meant to be a perfectly
objective or matter-of-fact account; it is an
old man's picture of the days of his youth. It
was written by Thucydides after the fall of
Athens, to try to show people what the Beloved
City really had been in the time of her greatness
under her greatest leader. There may well be
some idealization, but what is instructive to
us is the sort of ideal that Athens pursued, not
the question whether she reached it or not.

It is not at all the ideal that would suit present-day Berlin or Moscow; nor yet ancient Sparta, nor Rome, nor Babylon nor Jerusalem. It is modern and—in the strict sense of the word—Liberal, *Liberalis*, or in Greek ἐλευθέριος "fit for a Free Man", without fear or hatred or inward slavery.

Pericles begins by explaining that Athens is called a democracy, because the government is in the hands of the many, not of the few. The law secures equal justice for all; but that does not mean that men are all on a dead level. Some are better than others, and those who excel in any way are more esteemed and honoured. There are rewards and privileges for real merit, but not for mere rank or wealth. Poverty is never a bar: the poorest citizen has the right to take part in the Assembly and try to make his contribution to the guidance of his country. Again, life is free. No one in his private life is frowned at, or treated with intolerance if he chooses to live in a way different from the common. In public life, Athenians are restrained from doing wrong not by force or threats of force, but by a general spirit of respect for the laws, especially those laws that bring protection to the injured or helpless, and the unwritten laws of decency and honour which are felt by good men but not enforced

by any statute. "We Athenians have happy
lives", says Pericles. "All the riches of the earth
flow into Athens through our widespread commerce. We provide leisure, not mere idleness,
for the overtired." The whole style of Athenian
life is refined, and a general interest in art and
culture serves to drive dullness away. "Our
military training may in various ways be better
than that of our neighbours, but we never
exclude foreigners or try to prevent their seeing
or learning things that might be useful to them.
Our City throws itself open to the world." (There
was no 'iron curtain': no perpetual fear of
neighbouring cities, no plotting against them.)

"The Athenians love beauty, but have not
luxurious tastes; they cultivate the mind without
any loss of manliness." As to wealth, of course
it is useful for many good purposes; but it is
not with us a thing to boast about or to display.
No one in Athens need be ashamed of being
poor, unless indeed his poverty is due to lack
of industry and good work—then he well may
be. Unlike other cities, Athens expects every
citizen to take an interest in public affairs; and,
as a matter of fact, most Athenians have some
sense of public affairs. We believe in the value
of knowledge as a guide to action: we have
a power of thinking before we act and of acting
too, whereas many peoples can be full of energy

if they do not think, but when they reflect begin
to hesitate. We make friends abroad by doing
good and giving help to our neighbours; and
we do this not from some calculation of self-
interest but in the confidence of freedom and
in a frank and fearless spirit, "I would have
you fix your eyes upon Athens day by day,
contemplate her δύναμις—her potentiality; not
merely what she is but what she has the power
to be, until"—the phrase is even stronger in
Greek than in English—"until you become her
Lovers. Reflect that her glory has been built
up by men who knew their duty and had the
courage to do it. Make them your examples
and learn from them that the secret of Happi-
ness is Freedom, and the secret of Freedom,
Courage."

That, as Thucydides' memory paints the
picture, is what Athens in her flower once was,
Athens before the Great War or—as the last
phrase seems to show—at the start of the Great
War. It was a free and happy city, simple in
daily life but rich in culture and thought, tolerant
at home and open and unsuspicious in its dealings
abroad. It sought foreign friendships by helping
other cities in their times of need. No doubt
the picture is idealized; but the striking point
is the kind of ideal that is aimed at, an ideal
not quite like that of any other civilization

between that time and our own nineteenth or twentieth century. It was a Liberal civilization: free, tolerant and unprejudiced; highly cultured; and out of its abundance generous and helpful to the rest of mankind.

But the Great War had begun, and Thucydides describes unsparingly its effects—in the hope, he says, that his account may possibly be of use to statesmen of later times, if by chance a situation of the same sort should ever occur again. War, he says, takes away that abundance and leaves no room for generosity. War is a violent schoolmaster: it educates men in doing violence to one another. The war of which he speaks was on a great scale. It lasted on, it became more bitter, and it spread farther and farther. It became what we now call ideological: a war of revolutionary against conservative or, more nakedly, of poor against rich, or merely of clique against clique, irrespective of right and wrong. There were 'fifth columns' all over Greece; there were civil wars, hidden or open, everywhere. After ten years there came not exactly peace, but at least a great frustrated effort at peace, frustrated by the various wrongs and grievances created by the war itself and clamouring for a second and worse war to set them right. War, all in all, for twenty-seven years, with civil wars in its train.

And what effect has it all on that high, free-minded, liberal civilization of Athens? Thucydides tells us. The whole Hellenic world, he tells us, was shaken, every part of it being divided between the partisans of one or other of the two great cities. "Civil war", he says, more pervasive of daily life and consequently more treacherous and cruel than other war—"led to every form of wickedness throughout Greece." At each new crisis men strove to outbid their opponents "by the ingenuity of their intrigues and the atrocity—the word is literally 'the unthinkableness' or 'unguessableness'—of their revenges". Revenge became dearer to men than self-preservation. All moral values were transformed. Violence, frantic energy, successful treachery, were the things applauded; prudence, moderation, good faith suspected and despised. Party feeling was stronger than any bond of family or affection. (Children, I suppose, betrayed or denounced their fathers.) "That simplicity which is so large an element in nobility of nature, was laughed out of existence." The root cause of it all was *Arché*, the wish for 'domination', the unlimited craving for Power. We hear perhaps of no atrocities in Athens itself, but there was a lowering of all standards. In home politics power fell into the hands of "the most violent of the citizens"; towards other

communities Athens too fell a victim to this
lust for power, this *Arché*, which another Greek
author describes as "the wicked harlot who
makes city after city in love with her, to betray
them one after another to their ruin" (Isocrates
8. 103). Thucydides expounds its principles in
an imaginary dialogue between the corrupted
Athenians of the later war time, and their
victims in the neutral island of Melos. The
Melians have committed no offence, but their
island would be useful to Athens. The Melians
appeal to law, to established custom, to justice,
to man's regard for the gods; the Athenians
explain frankly that such considerations are
of no account to them; it is only Power that
matters. They use their power, conquer Melos,
kill the men, sell the women and children into
slavery, and therewith—the historian grimly
adds—they set off triumphant on the fatal
expedition against Sicily which is to bring the
reward of *Hubris* and leave imperial Athens
in the dust.

The great liberal Hellenic civilization failed
to get rid of war, and war was able to destroy
it—by inward poison as well as by outward
violence. Thucydides was perhaps not so far
wrong when he thought that his history might
be of some use to statesmen of later ages if the
same sort of situation should ever occur again.

V

THE HELLENISTIC AGE

THE PELOPONNESIAN WAR not only left Athens and her rivals in the dust, but led, as has often been observed, to a change in the direction of Greek thought. The fifth century had been the age of the Polis: a man's whole duty was towards his City; his pride and his hopes were centred in his City's greatness; the gods he worshipped were his City's gods; there was no greater glory than to die for his City. And now the City, with its claim for *Arché* over subjects and rivals and over the mind and conscience of its citizens, had calamitously failed. In the fourth and third centuries the interest of thought in Greece had turned from the service of the City to the good of Man and his soul.

The City died hard. It was the best form of society hitherto achieved. It did maintain a higher civilization than any mere collection of tribes or any slavish oriental empire. Demosthenes, with splendid eloquence and courage, tried hard to preserve Athens, with all her

faults, alive and free. Isocrates, perhaps the
wisest publicist of the time, took the same view
as Thucydides: it was not the City itself that
was wrong; it was the pursuit of that wicked
temptress *Arché*. Two of the great philosophers
held the same faith. Plato, who had suffered
bitterly through the whole age of baffled hope,
proletarian violence and ultimate defeat, kept
seeking always for some City that should be
guided right, should seek not Power but Justice,
and itself be Justice realized; perhaps the City
of a great philosopher king; perhaps something
more ordinary and prosaic, if only it could
have good laws and avoid the errors of the
mad Athenian demos. Aristotle more practically
analyses the necessary problems of the state
and, in order to have good material before
him, actually makes a collection of over a hundred—perhaps over two hundred—different
existing constitutions. But most of the great
fourth-century schools—Stoics, Pythagoreans,
Epicureans, Cynics, and devotees of the various
Saviour-religions—have turned away from the
consideration of worldly values and speak chiefly
of the soul and its duties, virtue, wisdom and
inward peace. And even Plato and Aristotle
seldom or never condescend to touch contempo-
rary politics.

As for *Arché*, that craving for power over

others, which in its simplest form is merely
an instinct of life and growth but may pass
so swiftly both in nations and leaders of nations
into the most ruinous of passions, it was already
condemned. It had been to Thucydides "the
cause of all the evils". Besides, the City-state
soon proved to be too small and weak a unit
to think of Empire; her highest hope now—
and that a precarious one—was to preserve
her own freedom. For *Archê* there were now
much larger units of power in strife with one
another; not mere cities, but whole nations,
or masses of barbaric tribes conquered and made
more efficient by Alexander's generals. His
successors found themselves in control of great
semi-hellenized empires, in which there was
a sharp difference between the Cities and the
Hinterland. The Cities had been hellenized:
there was Greek law; an accused person had
free speech and a fair trial; he knew what the
law was, and his punishment, if guilty, was of
a civilized sort. The vast Asiatic hinterland
had not yet been dealt with. There a king or
a native satrap could condemn a man without
trial; could invent his punishment; could, if
he liked, condemn the offender's whole family
with him. Outside the Cities, the Syrian empire
was still a place where, as a Greek poet puts
it, "heads are cut off, eyes gouged out, limbs

mutilated; where boys are castrated and the
air is filled with the groaning of men impaled
or crucified". Such an empire was still in the
main barbaric, but under its Greek rulers it
was eagerly trying to 'hellenize' itself and become
Greek. Indeed, the whole Mediterranean world
was trying. Intelligent or enterprising men set
themselves to copy Greek ways, to learn the
Greek language, to read Greek books, to listen
to Greek teachers and try to understand the
secret of Greek superiority.

These two or three centuries are known as
the Hellenistic Age; but it would be a mistake
to think of the process as a simple one, between
Greeks on the one side and mere 'barbarians'
on the other. There was a great meeting and
mingling of different cultures and traditions:
especially Hebrew, Syrian and Egyptian. But it
was Hellenistic for two reasons. For practical
purposes of business and diplomacy Greek had
become the necessary language, while in the
realms of the imagination and the intellect
there hung about all that was Hellenic an almost
uncontested aura of superiority. Men sought
to become 'hellenized', partly for reasons of
fashion or utility, but also because at a time
when races, customs and religions were mingled
and confused, Greek culture was not only held
to be the noblest but was also the most tolerant

and the least oppressive to new-comers in its rules and customs. The Jews, for instance, were esteemed as "a philosophic race", with their monotheism and their wonderful Book telling in an orderly way how the world was really made, not all in confusion like Hesiod. But there were difficulties in Judaism; narrow compulsory laws and customs; a great deal of prejudice and the permanent doubt whether full membership was open to any but children of Abraham. The Egyptians, again, had masses of ancient wisdom. They had in Isis and Osiris a religion which summed up the vegetation worships that were practised everywhere. Then they had minor figures, like the divine baby Harpocrates, who attracted wide sympathy. But then, their worship of animals, their lack of any freedom or enlightenment! No, of the various possible cultures Hellenism was by far the most attractive.

But to ape Greek habits was not to become Hellenic. It was easy for a barbarian to use Greek weapons and inventions, to practise Greek methods of commerce, to throw off a number of foolish taboos and superstitions, and yet to remain in heart and conduct a barbarian. Nay, if it comes to that, it was not difficult for a Greek in a barbarian world to be barbarized without knowing it. Antiochus IV was determined to

win the loyalty of his Asiatic subjects by hellenizing them as fast as possible. That policy landed
him in the hopeless barbarity of torturing and
perhaps executing Jews, not for any unlawful
act but in order to compel them to eat pork.
A Hellene barbarized might be worse than any
native barbarian, because the native, however
foolish, would have some rules that he must
not break; the Greek might well have come
to the conclusion that all moral rules were
superstitions. On the other hand, the mixture
of Hellene and barbarian, at its best, might be
something new and splendid. The Stoic school
itself was founded by an Asiatic, Zeno, who
had learnt and taught in Athens.

It was a strange confused age. Perhaps what
strikes one most is man's lack of control over
his environment. He wanted so much and
achieved so little. The successors of Alexander
had very large forces, but they could not keep
the sea clear of pirates nor even the roads of
robbers. The Greek cities were always making
arbitration treaties and praying for *Homonoia*,
Concord; but it always eluded them. They believed in Equality, but somehow fell into enormous
inequalities of wealth. Slavery is a typical case.
Philosophers were troubled in mind about the
whole institution, but it was far too strong for
them: it could not be changed without frightful

consequences. Neither Stoicism nor Christianity dared touch it. The New Testament says explicitly again and again: "Slaves, obey your masters"; and the philosophers, though they did not positively say the same, never said otherwise. Stoic, Pythagorean, Epicurean and the rest were content to treat slavery as a misfortune like any other; to make in their own minds no difference between slave and free, and to welcome into their spiritual communities on terms of equality all men, slave or free, male or female, who were seekers for the divine truth. There was an extraordinary output of idealist thought and ethics, Platonists, Stoics and followers of Epicurus all rejecting the values of the material world and concentrating upon higher things; an immense spread of the so-called Saviour-religions gathered round Osiris, Hermes the Mediator, Asclepius the Divine Healer, and others who professed somehow to deliver man-kind from "the body of this death". It is note-worthy that in our very imperfect records we frequently find individuals manumitting their own slaves by twos and threes, while the big world markets went on enslaving others by thousands. We hear of rich men doing wonders of generosity to help communities in distress; of doctors in times of pestilence giving up all fees, working night and day, and being rewarded

at the end by a wreath of olive and an inscription
which has happened to survive. We hear of
great sacrifices made to ransom prisoners; and,
in one case, of a man who gave himself up as
a prisoner to pirates as a substitute for two
captive women.

Hellenism in the true sense was open to all
who "sought wisdom". For wisdom was a thing
of the soul and open to every man. Part of the
wisdom, no doubt, was in the Hellenic culture
itself: to love and keep alive the works of the
old Greek poets and artists, creators of beauty,
and the understanding of the great philosophers,
seekers for wisdom and virtue. And, perhaps
most of all, to carry on that great continuing
effort by which Hellas had sought, in the words of
a Delphic inscription, "To tame the savageness of
man" and "to make gentle the life of the world".

Did they utterly fail? Well, failure and success
are relative terms and nothing human lasts for
ever. Amid much obvious failure, in two important points the hopes of the Hellenistic Age
were won. The leadership of the world fell not
to any barbarous power, but to the most Hellenic
of organized societies, to the city which had
sat most devotedly at the feet of the great Greek
writers and thinkers; which did produce once,
in Marcus Aurelius, a great Philosopher King,
and did achieve an epoch of world peace which

some historians have pronounced to be the happiest known period of human history. It is always worth remembering that Rome's Empire was not entirely won by force; that the Ptolemies, for instance, asked Rome to take over their dependency, Cyrene, for the good of the inhabitants; that Attalus of Pergamum thought he could best secure the freedom of his kingdom by making the Roman people his heir. And in the realm of the mind, it is a great thing that Rome did at least preserve a memory of something better than its own practice, an ideal Hellenism which can still in many ways be an inspiration to the world.

HELLENE AND BARBARIAN

IN THIS whole story—the pride of the "Beloved City"; the pursuit of *Archê* by each City separately, ending in general war and the ruin of all the Hellenic world; the gradual self-conviction of the City itself as a unit too small and weak to stand alone; the attempt of a barbarian world somehow to attain Hellenic culture without submitting to Hellenic rule; the persistent effort to obtain *Homonoia*, Concord, between City and City, nation and nation; the attempt of philosophic Athens to save what she most valued by turning from the failure of the individual City to the saving of mankind and its soul—is it fanciful to see in all this a strange likeness to the history of our own age? Is it not merely to recognize a fact of history? The continent of Europe has been our modern Hellas; her separate nations have been the independent Cities, and their wars her ruin, as the wars of Athens and Sparta were the ruin of Hellas. And surely we may without self-flattery claim that in the high civilization which

Europe has inherited and passed on to her kindred across the oceans, is a Hellenism which the barbarian rejects but still longs to understand and assimilate.

For many centuries Europe was supreme among the organized societies of the world, with settlements all over the other continents in which the white man, as a matter of course, gave orders and the coloured natives obeyed. He governed not merely by military and economic power, but because on the whole he knew how to govern, and when he did wrong was promptly criticized by his own people. He had more resources, more knowledge, better justice, higher culture, and more humane ways of life; he did not habitually breed to the famine limit, and he had overwhelming prestige. Europe was the heir to a grand inheritance. From Jerusalem she had her monotheism and her Old Testament, from Rome her law and government, from Greece the love of freedom, knowledge, beauty and political justice, and, as a special bond among all her nations, a small Greek book proclaiming a religion of love and the supreme value of the soul. For a long time she seemed to be generally true to her inheritance, progressing steadily towards peace and co-operation and the arbitration of all national differences, till suddenly in the early days of this century

the movement forward seemed to be reversed.
The actual increase of world unity, it would
seem, resulted in bringing about world wars.
The sovereign independent units in which the
world was organized had been brought close
together before they were ready for it: they
hurt one another, their ambitions clashed, and
the evil courtesan *Arché* proceeded to work her
will. It was war and more war, until, to use
Thucydides' words, "war gave rise to every
form of wickedness" throughout Europe, and
"each party tried to surpass his rival in the
ingenuity of his plots and the atrocity—or
'unthinkableness'—of his revenges". Are the
words not strangely apt?

The wars were chiefly in Europe, and as a
result the former Queen of Continents is de-
throned; no longer the strongest, no longer the
wealthiest and most secure; no longer capable,
after the unspeakable lies and cruelties of the
Second World War, of claiming to be recognized
as without question the most righteous or humane;
her sovereign nations shown up as being no
longer Great Powers but, just like the Greek
Polis, units too small to think of aggressive *Arché*
or even to stand securely on their own feet.
Western Europe in general, I think, has learnt
her lesson: she aims no longer at further *Arché*,
she is content merely to hold her present position

and even, in some special cases, to retreat. Like
Hellas, she is surrounded by much stronger
units of power, a terribly powerful enemy to
the east who rejects all her values, and an equally
powerful child to the west who loves and defends
them. Are we not indeed caught up in a great
Hellenistic Age in which Europe, however
weakened in force, still remains—with her great
ally in America—most advanced in knowledge,
in scientific technique, in the art of government;
in which some of her nations at least retain
undamaged her old standards of integrity and
public duty, while the outer world in other
continents, however rebellious against any claim
of superiority, however eager sometimes to take
advantage of her old masters when they are
down, is eagerly trying to master the methods
and secrets of Hellenism?

The general process seems to be beyond doubt.
Our Enemy Number One equips herself to
destroy European civilization with a creed
borrowed from a whole series of European
writers and with a technology devised by European mechanicians and inventors. China, in her
effort to become Enemy Number Two, is actually
turning away from the ancient Confucian traditions that were once her glory and adopting
the new-fangled doctrines of the German Marx
and the Russian Stalin. European civilization

has such prestige that the angriest non-Europeans
cannot do without it, and the best, while rejecting any *Arché* by the western world, have
powerfully embraced its Hellenism. In some
cases the blending of the two cultures, Hellenic
and non-Hellenic, has resulted in new values
which neither could have produced alone. We
may recall how the Phoenician Zeno, studying
in Athens, was founder of the greatest of Greek
schools of philosophy; has any religious teacher
of our time impressed the world, both east and
west, more than Mahatma Gandhi? In the
whole leadership of India today, both intellectual
and political, there is a rare blending of the
two great cultures; if only one could be sure
that it would last! It is a great disappointment
that the same has not happened in China.

The old Hellenistic world had, roughly
speaking, three great aspirations: it aimed at a
hellenizing or humanizing of the brutal world;
it longed and strove for *Homonoia*, Concord,
between community and community, between
man and man; lastly, it proclaimed a conception
of the world as One Great City, not of men
only but "of men and gods", which should on
the one hand supersede all local allegiances and
on the other should, like Plato's imagined Re-
public, be in itself an organization of the righteous
life.

The same aspirations are at work in the modern world, and before we call them vain we must reflect on the enormously greater power which, owing to two centuries of unparalleled scientific advance, lies in the hand of modern man and of modern organized society. Our first aspiration, like theirs, is *Homonoia*, Concord; and here, so far, we are defeated. Our two great international organizations, the League of Nations, and the United Nations, though effective beyond expectation in other ways, have certainly not produced world peace. How could they? They were meant to work in a world that was—or at least, taught by experience, wished to be— united, and instead have clashed against two terrible sources of disunion: first the strongest nations in the world drunken with the lust for *Arché*; and many large classes and even peoples in various parts of the globe eager to wreck the social order in order to overthrow their supposed enemies, domestic or national. The prospect is dark and presents our statesmen with the gravest of problems; but we notice that on the whole they preserve their unity, and that none of them has lost hope. Twice already, with the odds against us, we have won the day. It may be that our European Hellas is doomed still further to lose her prestige and her old leadership: it is possible, considering the enormous

world-wide sympathy is almost a new thing.
Nations used normally to be troubled by any
increase in a neighbour's wealth and strength:
now their normal practice is to help a neighbour's
poverty or weakness. The change is due chiefly,
no doubt, to our common fear; partly it is the
natural result of our increased powers of com-
munication and action. The suffering comes
close to us, therefore we feel; we know we have
the power to help, therefore we do help. Critics
often complain that this is an irreligious age,
and in many serious respects the charge is true.
Yet there is a religion, almost independent of
dogma, which seems to be stealing half-consciously
through the minds of men of different faiths
and nations when they face together the great
sufferings of mankind; a religion which men
really believe and on which they act. An old
Hellenistic phrase tried to express it: *Deus est
mortali mortalem iuvare:* "That man should help
his fellow-man is God", or should we say "is
man's nearest approach to God"? It is at least
in itself "true religion and undefiled". And of
that, I think, there is more in the world than
ever before.

GEORGE ALLEN & UNWIN LTD
London: 40 Museum Street, W.C.1

Auckland: Haddon Hall, City Road
Sydney, N.S.W.: Bradbury House, 55 York Street
Cape Town: 58–60 Long Street
Bombay: 15 Graham Road, Ballard Estate, Bombay 1
Calcutta: 17 Chittaranjan Avenue, Calcutta 13
New Delhi: Munshi Niketan, Kamla Market, Ajmeri Gate, New Delhi 1
Karachi: Haroon Chambers, South Napier Road, Karachi 2
Toronto: 91 Wellington Street West
Sao Paulo: Avenida 9 de Julho 1138–Ap. 51

by J. A. K. Thomson

THE ETHICS OF ARISTOTLE

Demy 8vo   18s. net

The Ethics is on the whole perhaps the most intelligible system of morals ever constructed by an original thinker. Yet, says Professor Thomson, more often than not a literal rendering of this great Greek classic results in a barely intelligible English. He has therefore attempted a translation in language familiar to modern readers.

THE CLASSICAL BACKGROUND OF ENGLISH LITERATURE

La. Cr. 8vo   2nd Impression   12s. 6d. net

"In so compressed a survey it would not be easy to say much that is new; Professor Thomson has wisely set out, first of all, to be fair and true. But he not only succeeds in this; he also makes, in passing, some points that will be new to many, and were well worth making."
The Classical Review

THE CLASSICAL INFLUENCE ON ENGLISH POETRY

La. Cr. 8vo   15s. net

"On the whole, balanced, informed and sensible, and he communicates to the reader the enjoyment he has clearly derived from writing this work." *The Listener*

"One of those books which I cannot imagine anyone reading without feeling enriched by it, also without feeling the need to read it again, slowly and studiously."
Poetry Review

by J. A. K. Thomson

THE ART OF THE LOGOS

La. Cr. 8vo   7s. 6d. net

"Uncommonly delightful . . . contains the most
persuasive and illuminating account I ever read of the
blending influences of art and history at a time when
they are just about to be torn asunder." *The Observer*

"Mr. Thomson has introduced, in previous books,
something new and vivid into the understanding of
ancient Greece. The study he has now made of the art
of story-telling in Greece, as exemplified by Herodotus,
will add to his reputation." *The Church Times*

SHAKESPEARE AND THE CLASSICS

La. Cr. 8vo   18s. net

There has been of late a revival of interest in the extent
of Shakespeare's indebtedness to the ancient classics.
As the question is one on which a classical scholar may
fairly be expected to offer an opinion, it has been re-
examined by Professor J. A. K. Thomson in this new
book. As a result of this study he has been led to make
two suggestions. The first is that the belief held about
Shakespeare by his intimates that he had not a scholarly
acquaintance with Latin or Greek has not been seriously
shaken. The second is that the tragic conception under-
lying Plutarch's *Life of Julius Caesar* was completely
grasped by Shakespeare, who was thereby enabled to
create a new kind of drama—Shakespearian tragedy—
which, owing nothing to the letter, owes a great deal
to the spirit, of Greek Tragedy.

GEORGE   ALLEN   AND   UNWIN   LTD